SUMMARY OF
EXTREME
OWNERSHIP
HOW NAVY SEALS LEAD AND WIN

BY

JOCKO WILLINK
AND
LEIF BABIN

Proudly Brought To You By
CONCENTRATE

WITH KEY POINTS
&
KEY TAKE AWAY

Disclaimer

This book is a summary and meant to be a great companionship to the original book or to simply help you get the gist of the original book. If you're looking for the original book, kindly go to Amazon website, and search for Extreme Ownership by Jocko Willink And Leif Babin.

Table of Contents

Table of Contents...3

Overview...5

Preface 8

Introduction: Leadership: The Single Most Important
Factor 13

PART I: WINNING THE WAR WITHIN...17

    Chapter 1: Extreme Ownership..17

        Important Takeaways 17

    Chapter Two: No Bad Teams Only Bad Leaders....................22

        Important Takeaways: 22

    Chapter 3: Believe..27

        Important Takeaways: 27

    Chapter 4: Check the Ego...31

        Important Takeaways 31

PART II: LAWS OF COMBAT 33

    Chapter 5: Cover and Move 33

        Important Takeaways: 33

    Chapter 6: Simple..41

        Important Takeaways: 41

    Chapter 7: Prioritize and Execute 46

        Important Takeaways: 46

    Chapter 8: Decentralized Command....................................50

        Important Takeaways: 50

PART III: SUSTAINING VICTORY 55

    Chapter 9: Plan..55

Chapter 10: Leading Up and Down the Chain of Command ..62

    Important Takeaways: 62

Chapter 11: Decisiveness amid Uncertainty 67

    Important Takeaways: 67

Chapter 12: Discipline Equals Freedom—The Dichotomy of
Leadership...70

    Important Takeaways: 70

Overview

The idea that Willink makes in the book, Extreme Ownership, is that a group is only as good as their leader. A true leader cannot lead alone; they require a group behind them that is focused on the goal. A leader can only be considered a good leader when their team reaches their goals on a regular basis.

Willink describes that the leader needs to be modest and realize once they had been incorrect. Possessing mistakes and developing a method to right any errors is fundamental to be a successful leader. Leaders must keep the ego at the door, and their agenda is entirely specialized in their group, they need to ignore their agenda. Willink's perception of a leader that is beneficial to their group as someone who can concentrate purely on the goal and bring the team together to reach that goal.

A thing that all leaders must remember is that you might be entirely responsible. All of it boils down to you. Willink explains that this responsibility is at the core to be a leader that works well with their team and recognizes the strengths of each member of the team. That is why he calls it extreme ownership – you need to acquire those things and results regarding the group behind you.

This duty applies to any successes, and any failures, it is not entirely all about the positive outcomes. A good leader must be ready to take the blame when things fail. The ability to acknowledge any failures, and realize mistakes is just a fundamental element of being a great leader. You then need to establish a method to fix any errors made. It is all down seriously to the leader and how they respond in all situations.

A weak leader = a group that is unable to attain success

Willink stresses that to be a true leader you need to make sure that your plans and tactics are straightforward and easy. Whenever things get complicated, individuals misunderstand, wires have crossed, and inevitably things fail. As the leader, you will need to communicate the plans and strategies as clearly as possible to ensure that everyone else understands every action. Recognizing where the weak point is and being able to prevent those gaps in understanding are essential.

The principle that is key Willink desires leaders to consider is you will want to prioritize and execute e.

Particularly, when under pressure. Pressure calls for leaders to be able to predict outcomes and anticipate dilemmas. Make it your goal as a leader to always be one step ahead. A leader can stay ahead of the target; they must be able to consider solutions to their issues before they also arise.

Another essential task of a great leader is the ability to recognize the ability to lead in others within the team. Willink calls these people junior leaders and he explains that it is critical that they are given an opportunity to lead so that the team advances together. If you do not recognize and consider the influential member of the team, you are rendering them worthless. Whenever a group that is primarily organized in this way, you can effectively lead a big group of people and reach success.

Preface

Important Take Away:

- **The Leadership Lessons Given in this book are learned through Combat Situations**
- **Leadership is about discovering your team as individuals**
- **Leadership is a transformation of yourself**

This book is not meant to take an individual's war tale and glorify it. You will see that the SEALs operate as a team. Each member is of high-caliber. The team is made up of multitalented individuals who have been through probably the most challenging and rigorous testing process anywhere. However, in the SEAL system, it is precisely about the Team. The team is only as good as the worst member.

This book describes SEAL combat = training through our eyes based on our perspectives. It is individual and unique as is our experience to leadership practices. Our SEAL operations were not based on what we had accomplished us as individuals; but rather our tales are associated with the SEAL platoon and task unit. Chris

Kyle, the SEAL sniper and composer of owner that is best US Sniper, which inspired the film, was one member of that platoon and task unit—Charlie Platoon's lead sniper and point man in Task Unit Bruiser. He played a component within the combat examples in this guide. Let's not forget that he wasn't alone. There was a bunch of other teammates who, though deserving of recognition, remain out of the spotlight. Not even close to being ours alone, the legislative war tales in this guide are regarding the Team as a whole unit. The combat scenarios describe precisely how we confronted hurdles as a combined group and overcame those challenges together. In the last end, there could be no leadership where there is entirely no team.

More than ten years of constant war and combat in Iraq and Afghanistan gave delivery to a new generation of leaders that begin to have a role in the ranks of America's fighting forces. These leaders had been forged not in classrooms through theoretical training and concept, but practical, real-life experience on the front lines of war. Leaders were tested in combat; ideas put through trials of fire. Across the ranks for the U.S. army solutions, forgotten wartime lessons were bloodstream that is rewritten—in. Some leadership maxims developed in training proved inadequate in actual combat. Hence, useful leadership abilities were honed while those that proved impractical were discarded. This created a spawning a new generation of combat leaders from across the full ranks of all of the U.S. military services was at the forefront with this leadership transformation, rising from the wins and trials of war with an understanding of what it will take to succeed in the complete, yet challenging environments that combat presence. Among this controlled chaos, new leaders will rise, and many war stories are born. After years of useful operations, like general operations that lead the raid that killed Osama bin Laden. U.S. Navy SEALs have been driven into the public's view. For the most part, it is attention than many never desired. This sudden attention has shed light on aspects of our company which few of us wanted to share. Any further in this book, we are careful never to remove that shroud. We usually do not discuss categorized programs or violate nondisclosure agreements surrounding our experiences that are functional — many memoirs that are SEAL been written—some by experienced and well-respected operators who wanted to distribute the heroic deeds and accomplishments of our tribe; a few, regrettably, by SEALs that has not added much towards the community. Like numerous of our SEAL teammates, we would have a view that is lousy SEAL publications have been posted. Why then would we choose to publish a book? As battlefield leaders, we discovered classes that are precious success and failure. We made mistakes and found from them, creating what works and precisely what does not. We taught SEAL leaders and viewed them implement the ideas we had seen with the exact success that is same difficult battlefields. Then, we once again saw the leadership maxims we then followed in combat lead to victory for the companies and executives we taught even as we worked with companies in the civilian sector. Numerous individuals have asked us to document our lessons learned in a concrete means so that other leaders can follow in our footsteps. We had written this book to capture those leadership axioms for future generations, to guarantee they might not be forgotten, so when wars which can be new and end such essential classes will be rewritten in the bloodstream. We penned this so that the leadership classes can continue to impact teams beyond the battlefield in every leadership situation—any business, group, or organization when a blended band of individuals strives to attain a goal and accomplish a mission. We wrote this written, book for leaders everywhere to make use of the axioms we discovered to lead and win. Who are we to print this type or form of writing? It may seem that anybody who thinks they could write a

guide on leadership must think on their own the epitome of what every leader should aspire to be. But our company is far from ideal. We continue steadily to discover and grow as leaders every, like any leaders who are genuinely truthful with on their must day. We were merely fortunate enough to experience a selection of leadership challenges that taught us lessons that are valuable. This guide is our effort that is best to share some essential skills. It is being told not from a pedestal or a position of superiority, but from a humble place, in which the scars of our failings still show.

Introduction: Leadership: The Single Most Important Factor

Important Takeaways

- **Management is the basis of leadership**
- **No two leaders are the same**
- **Effective Leaders learn from their team**

This guide is about managing situations. It entirely was written for leaders of groups small and enormous, for men and ladies, for just about any person who aspires to higher themselves. This guide is not any war memoir though it has new accounts of SEAL fight operations. Its instead of an accumulation of classes discovered from our experiences to help various other leaders achieve victory. If it is a guide that is useful

to leaders who aspire to develop, train, and lead high-performance teams which can be winning it has carried out its function. One of the legions of management publications in the book, we found focus. This is undoubtedly many on individual techniques and own personality traits. We also observed that lots of leadership that are business programs and administration consulting businesses do the same. But without a team— some individuals trying to accomplish a mission—there may be no leadership. Honestly, the only measure that is meant a leader is whether the group succeeds or fails. For all your meanings, descriptions, and characterizations of leaders, you can find only two that matter: inadequate and useful. Effective leaders lead active groups that accomplish their objective and win. Ineffective leaders try not to. The concepts and ideas explained in this written guide, whenever correctly recognized and implemented, allow any leader to be efficient and take over his or her battleground. Every leader and every organized group at some point or time will fail and must face that failure. That also is a part this is indeed huge of the guide. We have been by no means leaders who can be infallible no-one is, no matter exactly how skilled. No leader has every answer to every problem that could arise. We've made blunders being huge. Frequently our mistakes offered the best lessons, humbled us, and allowed us to grow better and become. For leaders, the humility to acknowledge and blunders being very own create a want to overcome all of them is important to success. The greatest leaders are not driven by pride or agendas that are private. They are merely focused on the objective and how best to accomplish it.

The lessons that have been laid out in this book are ones that were learned as SEAL leaders through our combined years of expertise are wide-ranging. For this guide, we have concentrated our efforts in the most critical aspects: the building this is indeed fundamental of leadership. The book derives its title from the principle—the that is first supplies the foundation for all your rest: Extreme Ownership. Leaders must own everything within their world. There is no one else at fault. Finally, "Sustaining Victory" covers the greater nuanced and difficult stability that leaders must navigate to be able to maintain the advantage and keep the team consistently perpetually running during the amount that is greatest. Each section is targeted on management this is indeed various, each unique though strongly associated and often mutually promoting. Within each chapter, you can find three subsections. The first identifies a management lesson learned through our U.S. Navy SEAL training or combat experience. The paragraph this is indeed 2nd that management concept. The third demonstrates the principle's application into the business community, based on a multitude to the work of organizations inside a wide range of sectors. We rely on these management concepts they work over and over, both in a fight plus in the company because we have seen. Their application this is undoubtedly correct and make certain effective leaders and teams that are high-performing produce extraordinary results. These principles enable those united groups to dominate their specific battlefields by allowing leaders to fulfill their purpose: lead and win.

PART I: WINNING THE WAR WITHIN

Chapter 1: Extreme Ownership

Important Takeaways

- **The Leader is responsible for the team's failures**
- **Recognizing responsibility is the beginning of Success**
- **Once the problem is identified, there must be steps to prevent a repeat**
- **Excuses are never an option**

All obligation to achieve your goals and accept failure in the responsibility of the leader on any staff, in just about any company. The top must have every little thing accounted for in their world. There is entirely no one else to blame. The leader must recognize mistakes and acknowledge failures, take ownership of those, and establish a plan to overcome them. Best leaders do not take responsibility just for their job. They merely take severe Ownership of everything that impacts their mission. This core that is fundamental enables SEAL leaders to guide high-performing groups in extraordinary conditions and win. But Extreme Ownership is not a concept whoever application is bound into the battleground. This notion may be the number-one characteristic of any excellent staff this is undoubtedly winning in virtually any armed forces product, organization, activities team or company team in almost any business. Whenever subordinates are not performing what they should, leaders that exercise Extreme Ownership cannot blame the subordinates. They must very first investigate a mirror at themselves. The leader holds duty this is undoubtedly full describing the strategic goal, developing the techniques, and acquiring the training and sources allow the group to properly and effectively perform. If a person on the united group is not doing at the amount required for the group to ensure success, the best choice must teach and mentor that underperformer. Then again, a leader whom workouts Extreme Ownership must undoubtedly be loyal to your team and the mission above anyone if the underperformer continually does not meet requirements. If underperformers cannot improve, the first choice must make the telephone call that is hard to terminate all of them and employ other people who will get the job done. It is all in the leader. As people, we quite often attribute the prosperity of other people to fortune or situations and work out excuses for our failures being own the shortcomings of your team. We blame the performance that is a lousy misfortune, circumstances beyond our control, or defectively carrying out subordinates—anyone but ourselves. The total obligation for failure is a thing that is tough to accept, and taking ownership when things go wrong needs extraordinary humility and nerve. But doing precisely that is a requisite this is indeed comprehensive understanding, growing to be a leader, and increasing a team's overall performance.

Extreme Ownership requires leaders to consider an organization's issues through the lens this is indeed unbiased of, without mental attachments to agendas or plans. It mandates that a leader ready ego aside, accept obligation for problems, assault weaknesses, and consistently work to build a better and much more group that is efficient. This type of leader but will not just take credit for their team's successes but bestows that honor upon their leaders that are subordinate associates. When a leader establishes this kind of instance and expects this from junior leaders within the United team, the mindset develops into the team's culture at each degree. With Extreme Ownership, junior leaders take control of the smaller groups and their bit of the mission. Effectiveness and effectiveness enhance exponentially as well as a high-performance, winning team could be the outcome.

No matter what company you are with, the ability to accept responsibility it the first step towards progress. You must see the problem the problem. Then you must be able to initiate the actions needed to keep the problem from repeating. No matter who is above you, you must realize that you are responsible for using the tools at your disposal.

The best-performing SEAL devices had leaders who accepted duty for everything. Every blunder, every failure or leaders that are a shortfall—those own it. Those good SEAL leaders took ownership of failures, sought assistance with how to improve, and identified an option to overcome challenges regarding the next version through the debrief after a training goal. The best leaders checked their egos, acknowledged blame, sought after criticism that is constructive and took detailed notes for enhancement. They exhibited Extreme Ownership so that as a total outcome, their

SEAL platoons and task devices dominated. When a SEAL this is undoubtedly a lousy leader into a debrief and blamed everybody else, that attitude was acquired by subordinates and staff users, who then implemented suit. All of them blamed everyone else, and inevitably the United team was ineffective and unable to perform a plan properly. Continuing, the VP had been told by me, "In those situations, you were left with a unit that never felt these people were at fault for anything. All they did was ultimately make excuses and never made the adjustments essential to fix problems. Now, compare that to the leader who arrived in and took the fault. He said, 'My subordinate leaders made bad calls; I must n't have explained the intent that is overall enough.' Or, 'The assault force didn't perform the way in which I envisioned; I have to make sure they better comprehend my intent and thoroughly rehearse more.' The leaders that are the best take ownership for the errors and shortfalls that occur. That's the difference this is undoubtedly crucial.

Chapter 2: No Bad Teams Only Bad Leaders

Important Takeaways:

- **A leader must prepare for anything**
- **A well-trained team can perform well even when the leader is absent**
- **It is essential to teach the team the standards that the leader expects**

The memoir of Colonel Hackworth's lengthy army career, combat experiences in Korea and Vietnam, hold the key to leadership lessons. Although a controversial figure later in life, Hackworth ended up being an excellent and battlefield leader that is highly respected. Into the book, Hackworth relates the viewpoint of his U.S. Army mentors who fought and defeated the Germans and Japanese in World War II: "There are not many units that are bad only bad officers." This captures the essence of exactly what Extreme Ownership is all about. It is a problematic and concept this is certainly humbling any leader.

Nonetheless, it is an essential mindset for creating a high-performance, winning team. When leaders begin to exercise the tips of Extreme Ownership they focus their teams on accomplishing a higher standard of performance; they need to recognize whenever considering criteria, as a leader, it is not what you preach; it's what you tolerate. Whenever setting expectations, regardless of what has been said or written, if poor overall performance is accepted and no one is held accountable—if there are no consequences—that poor performance becomes the standard that is new. Therefore, leaders must enforce rules.

Consequences for failing need not be straight away severe, but leaders must ensure that tasks tend to be repeated until the greater anticipated standard is achieved. Leaders must push the rules in a means that stimulates and makes it possible for the team to work with ownership that is severe. The top must pull the elements altogether to form the team and show them how to support one another. It enables them to be focused exclusively on how to accomplish the goal best. One lesson from the BUD/S watercraft crew leader example is that many people, like Boat Crew VI, desire to be part of staff this is certainly winning. They often do not understand how or need encouragement and motivation.

Teams need a function that is forcing the various members working together to achieve the mission. This is what leadership is about. Once a culture of Extreme Ownership is instilled into the team on every possible level, the teams entire performance goes on to enhance. You can count on the side even if the active leader is temporarily removed from the team. On the battlefield, being prepared for potential casualties plays a part that is key to a team's success, if a critical leader should go down. But life can throw any wide range of situations in the way of any business or staff, and every group must have junior leaders ready to move up and temporarily take on the roles and responsibilities of their instant employers to carry the team's mission on and get the job done if as soon as the necessity arises. Leaders should not be satisfied. They must continuously try to improve, and they must undoubtedly build that mindset into the group. They must face reality through a realistic, brutally truthful evaluation of themselves and their team's performance. Identifying weaknesses, great leaders seek to bolster all of them and think of a plan to conquer difficulties. The best groups anywhere, like the SEAL Teams, tend to be continually looking to enhance, add ability, and push the standards higher. It begins with the inpatient and spreads to each of the team users until this becomes the culture, the rule that is new. The recognition that there are not any groups which bad only bad leaders are facilitating Extreme Ownership and enables leaders to develop high-performance teams that dominate on any battlefield, literal or figurative.

Once you instill the concept of Extreme Ownership into the team at every level, the staff performance will continue to improve, even when a stronger leader is briefly eliminated from the staff. Regarding the battlefield, preparation for potential casualties plays a job that is critical of a team's success, if a vital frontrunner should go down. But life can toss a range of circumstances in the way of any business or team, and every group must have junior frontrunners willing to intensify and temporarily take regarding the roles and responsibilities of the immediate bosses to transport the team's mission on and get the job done if and if the need arises. Leaders must not be satisfied. They must always strive to improve, and all of them must build that mindset into the team. They must deal with the critical points via a realistic, brutally honest assessment of themselves and their team's performance. Identifying weaknesses, good leaders look to bolster all of them and think of a plan to conquer difficulties. The most useful teams everywhere, such as the SEAL Teams, are continually searching to improve, add capability, and push the requirements higher. It begins with all the individual and spreads to all the downline until this becomes the culture, the standard this is indeed new. The recognition that there are no teams that are bad only bad frontrunners facilitates Extreme Ownership and makes it possible for leaders to build high-performance teams that dominate on any battleground, literal or figurative.

Chapter 3: Believe

Important Takeaways:

- A Leader inspires others
- A leader understands the risks associated with an action
- A leader communicates his beliefs in the goal
- A leader is dedicated to the target because they believe in it.

A leader must undoubtedly be a true believer in the goal so that they can convince and inspire others to follow and accomplish an objective. Even when other people doubt and question the amount of risk, asking, "Is it worth it?" the leader must think in the more significant cause. When a leader is not dedicated to a goal, he or she will not take the changes necessary to get over the difficulties which can be inevitable to win. And they will not have the ability to convince others— especially the troops which are frontline must execute the mission —to achieve this. Leaders must always run aided by the understanding than on their own and their passions they are part of one thing better. They must impart this comprehension to their groups down to the tactical-level operators on the floor. Much more fundamental than training or equipment, a resolute belief in the mission is critical for any team or business to win and attain outcomes being huge. The leader must align their thoughts and eyesight to this of the purpose in many cases. When a leader thinks in the objective, that belief shines right through to those below and above when you look at the string of command. Actions and words reflect an idea by way of confidence this is undoubtedly evident self-assuredness which is not possible when hope is in doubt. The challenge comes when that alignment is not explicitly visible. When a trust this is indeed leader's, those that are meant to follow him or her see this and start to question their own belief into the mission. Every frontrunner must be ready to decide if the next task that is essential. They must understand how it will fit into strategic goals. When leaders receive an order, they must ask the concern: why that they question plus don't understand? Why are we being expected to work on this? Those leaders must take a step back. Take a good hard look at the problem, analyze the picture that is strategic and then arrives at a conclusion. Until they comprehend the reason why if they cannot determine a satisfactory answer on their own, they must make inquiries up the chain of command. If frontline leaders and troops realize why they can entirely move ahead believing in what they are performing. It is also incumbent on senior leaders to take the time and energy to describe and answer the questions of their frontrunners that are junior that they too can realize why and believe. The frontline troops never have as clear an awareness for the strategic picture as senior leaders might anticipate whether in the ranks of army units or companies and corporations. It is crucial that those senior leaders impart a broad understanding of the knowledge—the that is strategic their troops. In any business, goals must be in alignment always. This dilemma must be dealt with and rectified if targets are not aligned at some level. No senior executive team would purposely choose or issue a plan that would intentionally fail in business in the same way into the army. However, a subordinate may not understand a strategy that is certain therefore not have confidence in it. Junior leaders must ask questions and provide feedback up the sequence to ensure that senior frontrunners can fully understand the ramifications of how plans which strategic execution from the ground — belief in the realities in with the law that is fourth of Decentralized Command (chapter 8). The leader must describe maybe not how to proceed, but why. It may be the responsibility regarding the leader that is a subordinate reach away and ask if they cannot realize. Only when leaders after all known levels understand and believe in the mission can they pass that understanding and belief to their teams to persevere through challenges, execute and win.

Chapter 4: Check the Ego

Important Takeaways

- Your Ego can interfere with the goal of the team
- There is a difference between cocky and confident
- Humility is not a weakness

Ego clouds and disrupts everything: the look process, the ability to take good advice, and the power to accept criticism this is indeed constructive. It can also stifle someone's sense of self-preservation. Usually, the many egos that are difficult to deal with are your very own. Everyone has pride. Ego drives many people that are successful life—in the SEAL Teams, when you look at the armed forces, in the company globe. They desire to win, to be the best. This is certainly great. But when our ego clouds our judgment and prevents us from seeing everything the ego becomes destructive. Whenever individual agendas become more critical as compared to staff and the mission's that is overarching, performance suffers, and failure ensues. Lots of the problems being disruptive arise within any team could be attributed directly to a problem with pride. Acting on Extreme Ownership requires that you check your ego at the door. Admitting errors, taking ownership, and developing a plan to overcome challenges tend to be integral to any staff that is prosperous. Ego can prevent a leader from performing a genuine, realistic assessment of their very own performance and the performance of the group. In the SEAL Teams, we make it our goal to be confident, although not cocky. We take tremendous pleasure within the history and legacy of our business. We are sure in our skills and are also eager to take on missions that are challenging other people cannot or are not willing to perform. But we cannot previously to believe we are good to fail or that our enemies are not capable, lethal, and desperate to take advantage of our weaknesses. We must never get complacent. This is how controlling the ego is vital.

PART II: LAWS OF COMBAT

Chapter 5: Cover and Move

Important Takeaways:

- Teamwork means everyone working together
- The entire team operates together to maintain the focus of the mission
- Every person must work independently to create a perfect performance
- Each person is vital as an individual

Cover and Move is the primary tactic that everyone in the team must recognize. To simplify: Cover and Move means teamwork. All elements within the more team are especially important and must come together to accomplish the objective; They have the task of mutually supporting the other person, so the overall goal is achieved. Departments and groups inside the team must break down walls, depend on each other and realize who is dependent upon them. If they don't recognize this principle and learn to operate independently or work against each other, the results can be catastrophic to your team's performance. Within any united staff, some divisions arise. Often, when smaller groups within the team get so focused on their tasks that are immediate, they ignore what other people are doing or just how they rely on other teams. They might begin to contend with one another, as soon as there are hurdles, blame and hatred develop. This creates friction that inhibits the team's performance. This is undoubtedly overall. It drops on leaders to continually hold perspective on the mission this is indeed strategic remind the group that they are part of the higher team and the strategic goal is vital. Each user of the group is critical to success, although the effort that is main encouraging efforts must be identified. If the staff that is overall, everyone fails, regardless of if an individual user or a component within the team did their particular job successfully. Pointing fingers and blame that is placing

Other people contribute to dispute that is further teams and individuals. Him or her and organizations must find a way instead to work together, communicate with each other, and mutually support the other person. The focus must be on how constantly to best accomplish the mission. Alternatively, when the united team succeeds, everyone within and helping that team reaches. Every individual and every unified group in the larger organization gets to share in the success. Achieving the strategic mission could be the concern that is highest. Team members, divisions, and assets that are always supporting Cover and Move—help one another, work together, and help each other to win. This principle is vital for any united team to achieve triumph.

Jocko and I endured ahead of the class of a dozen midlevel managers seated at tables forming a U-shape inside a conference room regarding the company's corporate headquarters. In the 2nd session of a twelve-month program, this is undoubtedly leadership-training our presentation and discussion centered regarding the Laws of Combat. We solicited from every one of the class participants leadership that is specific they currently faced. Jocko and I set about to assist them in solving these difficulties through the effective use of the SEAL combat management principles they had just learned. The production supervisor explained that their team struggled to minimize downtime in their production—the times when they had to cease product this is undoubtedly making. These disruptions occurred for some reasons, nonetheless, they stopped the item from moving to promote, and every hour and day of downtime cost the company huge revenues and significantly impacted the line that is base. With his crew merely getting out of bed and running, there had been a learning curve that is steep. The production manager's staff maintained an downtime that is average was much worse than the industry standard. Such a glaring discrepancy had been a detriment that is major the company's profits. The production supervisor was under scrutiny and intense force to reduce downtime because of this. The subsidiary company on which his production staff depended became the scapegoat this is indeed significant blame. "We fork out a lot of your time waiting for us," said the production manager on them[the subsidiary company], and that causes big problems and delays. "Those delays are impacting production and costing our company serious income." "How are you able to help this subsidiary company?" Manufacturing ended up being asked by my manager. "I can't!" he replied. "They don't work for me. We don't work for the bosses that are same. They certainly are a various business." Which they were a unique business, both businesses dropped underneath the management of the identical mother or father corporation while he had been right.

"Besides," he added with indifference, "they aren't my problem. I've got my team. This is certainly very own to about."

"It sounds I responded like they truly are your trouble. "In that sense," he agreed, "I guess these are typical." "What's worse," continued the production manager, now on a roll of bashing the subsidiary business, "because corporate owns them, we are forced to make use of their services." "What you simply called the worst part must be the good thing," Jocko reacted. "You tend to be both owned by the same corporation, so you both have the objective that is the same. And that is what this is about—the overall mission, the team that is overall. Not merely your group, but the whole team; the whole corporation—all departments within your business, all subsidiary companies underneath the business, outside contractors, the enterprise that is whole. You must interact and support each other as one team." "The opponent exists," I said, pointing aside the screen to the world past. The enemy is any of the competing companies in your field that are vying for your customers. The opponent is not in here, inside the walls of this company. The divisions within and the subsidiary companies that all fall under the same leadership structure—you are all regarding the group that is same. You have actually to overcome the verses that are 'us' mentality and work together, mutually supporting one another." Exactly what he couldn't see exactly how his mission aligned with the remainder of the corporation and encouraging possessions, all striving to accomplish the same strategic mission as I had on the battlefield in Ramadi years before, the manufacturing manager was now so centered on his very own division and its immediate tasks. The production supervisor must now be ready to take a step back and see how their production team's objective fit into the general plan as I had done after some useful guidance from my chief. "It concerns the bigger, strategic goal," I said. "How could you help this subsidiary company do their task more effectively you accomplish your goal, and you can all win? So they really can help" The production manager pondered this. He had been still skeptical. "Engage with them," directed Jocko. "Build a relationship that is private them. Explain for them things you need all of them what can be done to help them enable you to get what you need from them and the reason why, and inquire. Cause them to the right part of the team, not an excuse for your team. Remember the whole tales Leif and I have told about relying on other devices to support us? Those Army and Marine Corps units we worked with are not under our control. We had employers that are various. But we depended they depended on us to them and with them and worked collectively to complete the overall mission of acquiring Ramadi, so we formed relationships. That's Cover and Move. You ought to do the one thing that is same: work together to win." The manufacturing manager had been a driven leader who wanted his team to perform at the level that is highest. Now, he began to understand teamwork this is certainly true. The proverbial light bulb went off inside the head, along with his mindset completely changed: then he was a deep failing his team if he wasn't working together with this subsidiary company. The production manager made every effort to positively engage using the subsidiary company, to communicate with them, and establish a better working over the next weeks and months relationship. He came to much more completely understand the difficulties that are myriad impacted their timelines and caused delays and what he could do on their end to help mitigate those problems. It ended up being not while he had initially surmised which they were "horrible. They were running with limited resources and workforce that is limited. Once he accepted which he and his staff could take to assist the subsidiary company to become more efficient and fill in gaps that had caused their delays that they weren't on to sabotage his staff, he recognized that there were steps. In place of being employed as two organizations which can be split each other, they started to interact. Manufacturing manager's encouragement enabled his area frontrunners to see the subsidiary business workers in a new light: never as adversaries but as critical resources part of the same greater team with this move in mindset. Most important, the production staff started initially to work utilizing the subsidiary company's field team. The production team's field leaders encouraged essential personnel from the subsidiary business to stay in on their coordination group meetings in just a few months. Quickly, the verses that are "us" mentality had all but disappeared. They had broken through the silos and no longer worked against each other. The production team's downtime radically improved to business leading amounts. They now worked together as one team—Cover and go.

Chapter 6: Simple

Important Takeaways:

- Keep it Simple

- Over-explaining things confuse people

- When possible use graphics to explain things

Combat, like anything in life, features basic levels of complexities. Simplifying as much as possible is vital to success. Whenever plans and orders are too tricky, people could not comprehend them. As quickly as things fail, and they inevitably do go wrong, complexity compounds problems that may spiral away from the hand into total catastrophe. Plans and orders should be communicated in a fashion this is quick, obvious, and brief. Everybody this is undoubtedly part of the mission must understand and comprehend their or her component into the purpose and what things to do in the eventuality of many contingencies that are most likely. Being a leader, it does not matter how good you feel you have offered the provided information or communicated a purchase, plan, tactic, or strategy. Should your group have it, you have got not held things quick, and you have failed. You require to brief so your denominator that is lowest this is undoubtedly common the staff knows. It is essential, because really, that the operating relationship enables the capability associated with soldiers that are frontline ask concerns that clarify when they do not comprehend the goal or jobs that are crucially performed. Leaders must motivate this communication and take only the time that is right power to explain so that every user about the team knows. Simple: this principle is not on a battleground. In a business that is continuing, and in life, you will find inherent complexities. It is critical to keep plans and interaction simple after this guideline is imperative to the success of any united team in almost any fight, life or company.

The way in which is far better make your bonus plan work is to return into the drawing board and work to create a brand-new model for compensation, with two or three—no more than four—areas to measure and grade upon." The engineer that is primarily the plant manager accepted the goal I outlined for all of them and headed back to their office to get to work. The day that is next I stepped into the workplace. The plan ended up being had by all of them written up to their dry-erase board. It had only two parts: (1) weighted units; (2) quality. "That's it?" We inquired, this right time without sarcasm. "That's it," the plant manager replied. "Very easy. You supply as many units as time will allow. We will still adjust the weights of this device based on demand, but we will set the weights on and allow them to stay there until Friday Monday. That nonetheless provides us time the next few days to adjust and modification weights if demand spikes for a unit that is certain. And now we are likely to post the weights of every device out there on the bulletin board so that every employee in the relative line sees it, knows it, and it is considering it. The quality piece we are going to determine each month. Anyone with an excellent score of ninety-five % or maybe more will get a fifteen percent rise in their particular bonus." "I replied like it. This plan ended up being much easier to communicate and much better to understand. "When you need certainly to adjust it, you'll be able to do so with ease." That, I watched as the principal engineer and the plant supervisor discussed the plan utilizing the team leads and the afternoon shift mid-day. The response was great. Viewed as the chief engineer and the plant manager discussed the program with the team leads and the shifting afternoon. The answer was great. The employees now had a knowing that is great of it ended up being they needed to do to earn their particular bones. The new now indeed incentivized behavior and may, therefore, result in the company more productive as a result. The plant manager and chief, professional reported an almost immediate increase in productivity in the coming months. Even more, employees focused their power on what product would make them more money, which was of training course lined up with the goals of this business. Some impacts are additional well. The lower-producing workers were left with fewer orders to satisfy as the higher-producing employees strove harder to increase their bonuses. In just a month, the organization let go the four employees with the other scores that are lowest, who had long been the weakest performers along with dragged the complete team down. Now, the ongoing business no longer needed all of them, while the remaining portion of the crew had considerably increased their performance. The absolute most thing that is impressive this enhancement in performance was that it did not come from a significant process modification or an advance in technology. Instead, it came by way of a leadership concept which has been around for a long time: Simple.

Chapter 7: Prioritize and Execute

Important Takeaways:
- Do not Micromanage
- Decide what steps need to come first
- Create your plan of action
- Communicate your idea in a simple way
- Stick to your plan

Every challenge has its complex footprint, each demanding interest on the battlefield, countless problems compound into a snowball effect. But a leader must continue to be peaceful and make the best this principle with this direction: "Relax, look around, make a call." Even the most experienced of leaders can be overwhelmed if they decide to try to tackle too many projects at the same time. The group will fail at each likely of the tasks. Alternatively, frontrunners must determine the priority and a plan to execute it. When you feel like you are being overwhelmed, use this principle: Prioritize and Execute. Multiple issues and high-pressure, high-stakes environments are not exclusive to combat. They occur in many facets of life and particularly in company. Company choices may lack the immediacy of death and life, but the pressures on business leaders are nevertheless intense. The success or failure for the team, the department, the business, the capital that is financial of, jobs, and livelihoods are at stake. These pressures produce demand and stress choices that often require rapid execution. Such decision-making for leaders could be daunting. A implies that are particularly efficient assistance Prioritize and Execute under pressure is to keep at least a step or two forward of real-time problems. A frontrunner can anticipate likely challenges that could occur during execution and map away an effective response to those difficulties before they happen through careful contingency planning. That leader and his or her group are a lot more prone to win. Keeping ahead of the frontrunner is prevented by the curve from being overwhelmed when force is applied and enables greater decisiveness. Then rapidly execute whenever those problems arise, even without specific way from leaders if the team has been briefed and knows what activities to take by such likely contingencies, the group can. This may be a crucial characteristic of any high-performance, winning team in any business or industry. Also, it enables Decentralized that is efficient When confronted with the enormity of operational programs while the micro-terrain that is intricate those plans, it becomes an easy task to get lost in the details, to become sidetracked or shed focus on the bigger effort. It is essential, particularly for leaders towards the top associated with business, to "pull themselves off the firing line," step straight back and maintain the photo that is strategic. This is necessary to assist precisely prioritize for the group. With this perspective, it becomes far more straightforward to determine the priority effort. This is undoubtedly highest and focuses all energies toward its execution. Then frontrunners that are senior help subordinate the team leaders within their team focus on their efforts. Just as in combat, priorities can shift and alter rapidly. If at some point, leadership changes or in unavailable, the team should be able to communicate to each other. There should be no gaps in communication, no matter where the member is on the chain on command. Groups must be careful to avoid target fixation for an issue this is indeed single. They cannot fail to recognize when the priority task shifts that are highest to anything else. The team must maintain the capacity to reprioritize attempts and quickly adapt to a battlefield rapidly. This is indeed continually changing. A leader must implement Prioritize and Execute in any company, team, or company

Evaluate the priority problem that is highest — layout in simple, clear terms in order of highest priority effect for the team. Then create a game plan from input from crucial leaders and through the staff where feasible. Communicate the direct method for implementing a solution, focusing all efforts and sources toward this concern task. Move to the next highest priority problem. Repeat. When priorities shift inside the team, communicate the situation to both the upline and downline. Don't let the focus on a single target cause you to lose sight of the overall objective. Maintain the ability to see other dilemmas developing and shift as required rapidly.

Chapter 8: Decentralized Command

Important Takeaways:

- Create smaller teams
- Designate team leaders
- Communicate each teams goal
- Outline how each team's goal affects the overall goal

Humans are generally not capable of managing a lot more than six to ten people, particularly when things go sideways and contingencies which are unavoidable. Nobody leader this is certainly senior be anticipated to manage dozens of an individual, much fewer hundreds. Teams must be damaged on to manageable components of four to five operators, with a designated leader. Those leaders must understand the mission that is overall and the ultimate goal of that mission—the Commander's Intent. Junior leaders must be empowered to help make decisions on key tasks necessary to accomplish that mission within the best and manner this is certainly efficient. Teams within teams tend to be organized for maximum effectiveness for a mission. This is certainly particular with leaders that have delineated duties. Every team that is tactical-level must understand maybe not precisely what to complete but why they are doing it. If frontline frontrunners do perhaps not understand why they must ask their boss to clarify why. This ties in very closely with Believe (part 3). Decentralized Command does not always mean junior leaders or associates function to their system that is own results in chaos. Rather, junior leaders must grasp what's in their authority—the that is decision-making"left-right limits" of their particular responsibility. Every team member must communicate with senior leaders to suggest decisions outside what they feel is their range. This is so that their so the leaders can make well-informed strategic decisions. SEAL leaders from the battlefield are expected to find out just what has to be done and do it—to tell higher authority whatever they plan to do, rather than ask, "What do you want myself to do? junior leaders who are must certainly be proactive rather than reactive. To be effectively empowered to help make choices, it is imperative that frontline leaders execute with self-confidence. Tactical leaders must be confident that they comprehend the mission that is strategic Commander's Intent. They will need to have trust that their senior leaders will support their decisions. Without this trust, junior leaders cannot confidently execute. To make certain this is the case; senior leaders must continuously communicate and share information with their leaders being subordinate. Likewise, junior leaders must press situational awareness within the chain to their senior leaders maintain them informed, especially of crucial information that affects decision making that is strategic. With SEAL Teams—just much like any united team in the business world—there tend to be leaders who make an effort to take on an excessive amount of themselves. If this occurs, functions can dissolve into chaos quickly. The fix is to empower frontline leaders through Decentralized Command and ensure they are running their teams to support the goal that is totally without micromanagement through the top. There are. Likewise, other leaders being senior are so far removed from the troops executing regarding the frontline which they become ineffective. These leaders might provide the look of the control, but they really have no basic idea what their troops are doing and should not effectively direct their groups. This trait is called by us"battlefield aloofness." This attitude produces a disconnect that is significant leadership and the troops, and this type of leader's team will struggle to effortlessly accomplish their objective. Deciding how much leaders must be included and where leaders can position that is best themselves to command and control the group is key. When SEAL task devices train in assaults—in what we call close-quarters to struggle or CQB—we practice this in a "kill house." A kill home is a center this is certainly multiroom ballistic wall space, which SEALs, another military, and authorities units use to rehearse their CQB skills. For young SEAL officers learning the ropes of leadership, running right through the kill residence because of the platoon provides training that is great for ascertaining how much they should be involved and where to position by themselves. Often, the officer gets therefore far forward he is constantly entering rooms and engaging targets which he gets sucked into every area clearance, definition. Whenever that takes place, he gets focused regarding the minutia of what's happening in the room that is immediate loses situational knowing of what is occurring along with the rest of the team and will no longer provide effective demand and control. Other times, the officer gets stuck in the relative back of the train, on cleanup duty. When that occurs, he is too much into the backside to know what is happening up can't and front direct his attack power. I advised numerous officers that the right amount of involvement—the proper position for them—was somewhere in the middle, generally speaking using the almost all their force: not very far forward that they don't understand the proceedings up front that they get sucked into every room clearance, but maybe not thus far back. Contrary to a standard misconception, leaders are not trapped in every place this is certainly certain. Frontrunners must be no-cost to

proceed to where these are typically most required, which changes through the span of a surgical procedure. Understanding positioning that is proper a leader is a crucial element of effective Decentralized Command, not merely on the battleground. The same rule applies to any team, business, or company. The potency of Decentralized Command is crucial to the prosperity of any team in virtually any industry. In chaotic, dynamic, and environments which are rapidly switching leaders after all amounts must be empowered to create choices. Decentralized Command is an element that is a key victory.

PART III: SUSTAINING VICTORY
Chapter 9: Plan

Important Takeaways:

- Analyze the mission.
- Identify personnel, assets, resources, and time available.
- Decentralize the planning process. — Empower key leaders
- Determine a course
- Plan for likely contingencies through each phase regarding the procedure.
- Mitigate risks that may be controlled whenever possible.
- Delegate portions
- Continually check

What is the mission? Preparation begins with an objective evaluation. Frontrunners must identify directives that are unmistakable the group. After they understand the goal, they can impart this knowledge to their frontrunners which can be essential frontline troops tasked with carrying out the objective. A mission that is uncertain in the absence of focus, ineffective execution, and goal creep. To prevent this, the purpose should be carefully processed and simplified so that it is apparently clear and especially centered to achieve the greater vision that is strategic which that goal is a part. The target must explain the purpose this is indeed overall desired rest ult, a or "end state," of the procedure. The troops that are frontline with executing the objective must comprehend the deeper purpose behind the mission. The Commander's Intent is the important part of the brief during an easy statement. Whenever grasped by everyone else involved in the execution associated with the plan, it guides each action and decision on the ground. Different programs of action must be explored how best to achieve the mission—with the workforce, resources, and possessions that are encouraging. Once a strategy is determined, further preparation needs detailed information gathering to be able to facilitate the development of an agenda that is thorough. It is advisable to utilize all assets and slim regarding the expertise of these into the position this is certainly best to provide the absolute most accurate and current information. Leaders must assign the planning procedure down the chain as much as possible to crucial leaders being subordinate. Leaders must have ownership of their tasks inside the plan. This is certainly overall mission. Team participation can help to produce bold, revolutionary solutions to problems. Providing the frontline troops ownership of a good tiny piece of the plan provides them buy-in, helps them comprehend the causes of the plan, and better enables them to think in the goal, which means more execution that is effective execution from the surface. The whole planning process by associates, he or she should be mindful not to get bogged down in the main points while the senior leader supervises. The senior leader can better ensure conformity with strategic objectives by maintaining a perspective over the micro terrain regarding the plan. Doing so enables senior frontrunners to "stand back and be the genius"—to that is tactical weaknesses or holes in the program that those immersed in the details may have missed. This enables leaders to fill in those spaces before execution.

Once the plan that is detailed been developed, it should then be briefed to the entire team and all participants and supporting elements. Leaders must very carefully prioritize the given information to be presented in an accessible, clear, and concise a format as possible, so that team members do not encounter information overload. The planning procedure and briefing should be a forum that encourages discussion, questions, and clarification. The team's ability to effectively complete the plan significantly decreases if leaders are uncertain about the project and yet are also intimidated to ask questions. Thus, leaders must ask questions of their forces, encourage interaction, and ensure their teams understand the idea. Following a brief, this is undoubtedly effective for all members taking part in operation will follow the strategic mission, the Commander's Intent, the specific objective of the team, and their roles within that objective. They'll realize challenges that are contingencies—likely might arise and exactly how to respond. The test for the brief that is successful easy: Do the group and the supporting elements understand it? The plan must mitigate identified dangers where possible. SEALs are known for taking a risk this is undoubtedly significant however in truth SEALs calculate danger exceptionally carefully. An excellent plan must allow the opportunity that is greatest of goal success while mitigating just as much threat as possible. Some risks just cannot be reduced, and leaders must instead focus on those dangers that really can be managed. Detailed contingency plans help handle risk because everybody active in the execution that is a director in help) for the operation understands what to do when obstacles arise, or things go wrong. But whether regarding the battlefield or into the continuing business world, leaders must be comfortable accepting some standard of threat. As the U.S. Naval hero regarding the American Revolution and Father of the U.S. Navy, John Paul Jones, said: "Those who will not risk cannot win."2 The most readily useful teams use constant analysis of their particular tactics and measure their particular effectiveness to ensure that they can confirm their methods and use lessons learned for future missions. Often business teams claim there is the time that is n't such analysis. But one must make time. The best SEAL units, after every combat operation, conduct what we called a "post-operational debrief." In spite of how exhausted from an operation or how planning that is busy the next mission, time is right for this debrief because lives and future mission success be determined by it — an interrogation that is post-operational, all phases of operation from planning through execution, in a concise format. It covers the next for the fight objective just completed: What went right? Exactly what went wrong? How do we adjust our tactics even to make us more effective and increase our advantage over the enemy? Such self-examination permits SEAL devices to reevaluate, enhance, and refine what worked and just what didn't make sure that they can continuously improve. It is crucial for the accomplishment of any team in any business to complete similarly and apply those changes into their plans so they don't repeat the mistakes which can be the same. While companies might have their particular own planning process, it should be standardized so that other departments within the company and promoting assets beyond your organization (such as service technicians or subsidiary organizations) can understand and use the format that is the same terminology. It must be repeatable and supply users with a checklist of all the things that are important need to think

About. The master plan must be briefed to the participants, tailored toward the frontline troops charged with execution, so they realize it. Implementing such a preparation procedure will make sure the amount this is indeed highest of performance and present the team the best chance to accomplish the mission and win. A checklist that is the leader's preparation ought to include the next following:

Chapter 10: Leading Up and Down the Chain of Command

Important Takeaways:

- Take responsibility
- If someone is not doing what you need or need them to do, find out how you can change your leadership to reach them
- Do not ask your leader just what you should do, tell them what you may be planning to do.

Any good frontrunner is immersed in the planning and execution of tasks, projects, and operations to go the team toward a goal that is strategic. Such frontrunners possess an understanding of a more magnificent image and why functions which are specific is carried out. This information does not routinely translate to subordinate leaders and the soldiers that are frontline. Junior members of the team—the level this is undoubtedly tactical rightly focused on their specific jobs. They must be to accomplish the mission this is undoubtedly tactical. They do not need the data that is full insight of their senior leaders, nor do the senior frontrunners need the intricate knowledge of the tactical level providers' jobs. Still, it is vital that each have an understanding of the role that is others. And it is paramount that senior frontrunners reveal to their junior leaders and troops executing the mission how their part contributes to picture success that is big. This isn't intuitive and does not as obvious to the workers who can be rank-and-file leaders might assume. Leaders must routinely communicate using their team members to help them comprehend their role in the mission that is overall. Frontline leaders and troops may then connect the dots between whatever they do every day—the operations—and that is day-to-day that impacts the company's strategic goals. This understanding helps the team members prioritize their attempts in a rapidly altering, dynamic environment. That is leading down the string of demand. It requires regularly stepping from the office and personally engaging in face-to-face conversations with direct reports and observing the troops being a frontline activity to understand their unique difficulties and read them into the Commander's Intent. This enables the united team to understand why they are doing what they're performing, which facilitates Decentralized Command (as detailed in chapter 8). Like a frontrunner using ownership that is severe if your team isn't doing what you need all of them to do, you first need certainly to view yourself. Rather than blame all of them for not seeing the strategic picture, you must figure a way out to better communicate it to all of them in terms that are simple, visible, and concise, so that they understand. This might be what leading down the chain of command is all about.

In the event, the boss isn't deciding in a manner that is timely providing necessary support for your team, don't blame the boss. First, blame yourself. Study what you could do to communicate better the information that is important decisions to be made and support allocated. Leading up the chain of command needs engagement this is certainly aware the immediate boss (or in army terms, higher headquarters) to get the decisions and help necessary to enable your team to achieve its mission and eventually win. Doing this, a leader must push awareness that is situational the chain of command. Leading up the string takes so much more skill and savvy than leading straight down the chain. Leading up, the leader cannot fall right back on his or her positional authority. Instead, the subordinate leader must use impact, experience, knowledge, communication, and maintain the professionalism that is highest. While pressing to make you understand that is superior what need, you must also recognize that your employer must allocate limited assets making decisions using the bigger picture in the head. You and your staff may well not represent the priority effort at that time that is particular. Or perhaps the senior leadership has chosen a direction that is different. Have the humility to know and take this. One of the more important jobs of every leader is always to support your boss—your management that is instant. The leadership must constantly present a united front to your troops in any chain of command. A display that is public of or disagreement with all the chain of command undermines the authority of leaders at all levels. This is catastrophic to your overall performance of every business. As a leader, you have to ask those concerns within the string if you don't realize why decisions tend to be being made, requests denied, or assistance allocated elsewhere. Then, when understood, that understanding can be passed by you down to your team. Leaders in almost any chain of command shall not constantly agree. But at the end of a single day, once the debate for a course that is certain of has ended plus the boss has made a decision—even if that choice is one you argued against—you must execute the master plan as though it had been your own. When leading the people that are higher than you, use respect and care. But keep in mind, if your leader is certainly not giving the support you will need, don't blame her or him. Instead, reexamine what you could do to clarify better, teach, influence, or convince that person to provide you the thing you need to win. The factors that tend to be major be aware of when leading up-and-down the chain of demand are these:

Chapter 11: Decisiveness amid Uncertainty

Important Takeaways:

- Look at all Outcomes

- Decide which risks are to be avoided

- Look at the big picture

- Do not second guess your plan

Books, flicks, and television shows can never undoubtedly capture or articulate the pressure from doubt, chaos, and the factor of unidentified with which combat that is genuine must contend. The combat leader hardly ever gets the picture that is full a clear and certain knowledge of the enemy's actions or reactions, nor perhaps the knowledge of the immediate effects for momentary choices. The very first recognition of an attack might be the bad snap and violent impact of incoming rounds, flying shards of concrete and debris, or the screams of pain from wounded comrades on the battlefield, for all those immersed into the action. Urgent questions arise: Where will they be shooting from? How many are there? Tend to be any of my males wounded? If so, exactly how badly? Where are other forces that are friendly? answers tend to be hardly ever immediately apparent. The responses to who attacked and exactly how will never be understood in many cases. Regardless, leaders can't be paralyzed by fear. That leads to inaction. It is critical for all team leaders to act with direction amid doubt; to make the greatest choices, they can base on only the knowledge that is instant. This realization is one of the biggest lessons learned for our generation of combat leaders— in both the SEAL Teams and throughout other U.S. military branches—through the total several years of combat in Iraq and Afghanistan. No 100 percent solution 's right. The image is never complete. Leaders should be confident with this and start to become able to make decisions immediately, then be ready to adjust and make decisions quickly based on developing circumstances and information that is brand new. Intelligence gathering and study are important, but they must certainly be used with realistic expectations and must not hinder choice this is certainly swift that is often the difference between victory and defeat. Awaiting the 100 percent right and answer that is sure to delay, indecision, and an inability to execute. Leaders should be prepared to make an educated guess based on previous experience, knowledge of how the opponent operates, as the outcomes, and whatever intelligence is available in the minute this is certainly immediate.,

Chapter 12: Discipline Equals Freedom—The Dichotomy of Leadership

Important Takeaways:

- confident but not cocky

- courageous but not foolhardy

- competitive but a gracious loser

- attentive to details

- strong but have endurance

- a leader and follower

- humble not the passive

- aggressive not overbearing

- quiet, not silent

- calm but not robotic

- logical but still show emotions

Every leader must go a line that is good. That's precisely what makes leadership so challenging. Just as discipline and freedom tend to be opposing forces that must be balanced, leadership requires finding the equilibrium in the dichotomy of numerous qualities that are seeming, contradictory between one extreme and another. The recognition that is quick of is one of the most potent tools a frontrunner features. A leader can help to create a balance between opposing forces and lead with maximum effectiveness being mindful of this. A leader must also lead but be willing to follow. Sometimes, another member for the team— perhaps a subordinate or direct report—might be in a better position to produce a plan, come to a decision, or lead through a scenario that is particular. Possibly the person that is junior greater expertise in a specific location or more knowledge. Perhaps he or she just considered a much better way to perform the mission. Good leaders must welcome this, putting aside pride and personal agendas to ensure that the team has the opportunity this is indeed best of accomplishing its strategic goals — a frontrunner that is true maybe not threatened when others step up and take charge. Frontrunners that are lacking self-confidence in themselves fear being outshined by someone else. Then recognition will come for those in cost, but a frontrunner should perhaps not look for that recognition if the team is successful. A frontrunner needs to be confident adequate to follow another person as soon as the situation calls for it.

A leader must be strong but not overbearing. SEALs are known for their eagerness to undertake tough challenges and accomplish some of the most missions that are difficult. Some might even accuse me of hyper-aggression. But I did my utmost to guarantee that everybody else with concerns, ideas, thoughts, and even disagreements below me when you look at the chain of command felt comfortable approaching me. With concerns and present an opposing view if they thought anything was wrong or thought there was an easy method to execute, I encouraged them, regardless of ranking, in the future to me. I listened to all of them, discussed new options, and came up to a conclusion if it made sense together with them, often adapting some part or possibly even all of their idea. A leader must be peaceful yet not robotic. It is normal—and tv show emotion that is necessary—to. The team must take into consideration that their leader cares about them and their well-being. But, a strong leader must control their reactions and feelings. Or even, how can they expect to manage anything else? Frontrunners who lose their temper also lose value. But, at the time this is certainly the same to prevent show any sense of anger, sadness, or disappointment would make that leader appear without having emotion at all—a robot. Men and women do not follow robots. A frontrunner must be confident but never cocky. Confidence is contagious, an attribute that is great a leader and a team. However, when it goes too far, overconfidence causes complacency and arrogance, which ultimately set the united team up for failure. A frontrunner must be brave yet not foolhardy. He or she must accept work and risk courageously but must not be reckless. It is a job that is the leader's always mitigated as much as you can those risks that can be controlled to accomplish the objective without sacrificing the group or excessively expending vital sources. Frontrunners must possess a spirit that is competitive also be gracious losers. They must drive the competition and push themselves and their teams to perform at the degree this is certainly highest. Nevertheless, they must never put their drive that is own for success ahead of total mission success for the more team. Leaders must work with reliability and recognize others for their particular contributions. A frontrunner must certainly be conscious of details but not obsessed by them. A leader this is certainly good maybe not get bogged down in the minutia of a tactical problem at the cost of strategic success. He or she must monitor and always check the team's progress in most tasks that are important. But that leader cannot get sucked into the details and track that is lost of problem.

A frontrunner must likewise be powerful but have stamina, not only actually but mentally. He or she must maintain the power to perform at the particular level. This is certainly the greatest and sustains that level for the long term. Frontrunners must recognize limitations and know to pace themselves and their groups so that they can maintain an overall performance that is solid. Leaders must be humble, not passive; quiet but not hushed. They must possess humility and the ability to control their ego and listen to other individuals. They have to acknowledge errors and failures, take ownership of them, and figure out a real way to avoid them from happening once again. But a leader

must certainly be able to speak up when it matters. They must be able to stay up for the group and respectfully push back against a decision, order, or path that could adversely impact mission success this is certainly total. A frontrunner must be close with subordinates but not also close. The greatest frontrunners understand the motivations of the team people and know their people—their lives and their people. But a leader must never close grow therefore to subordinates that one member of the team becomes more important than another, or much more important as compared to the mission itself. Leaders must never get so close to their team that they forget just who is in control. A leader must exercise Extreme Ownership. Simultaneously, that leader must employ Decentralized Command by giving control to subordinate frontrunners. Eventually, a leader has nothing to prove but every little thing to prove. The group realizes that the frontrunner is within charge by rank and position. A leader that is good not gloat or revel in their position. A leader's authority is the mark of poor, inexperienced leadership lacking in confidence to take charge of minute details merely to show and reinforce to the group. A leader has nothing to prove since the team knows that the leader is de facto in charge, due to that. But new respect, a leader has everything to show: every member of the group must develop the trust and self-confidence that their leader will exercise judgment that is good remain relaxed, and make the right choices when it matters most. Leaders must earn that value and prove by themselves worthwhile, demonstrating through action that they will be mindful of the team and look on for his or her interests that are long-term wellbeing. A frontrunner has every little thing to show every single day for the reason that value. Beyond this, many other leadership dichotomies must be carefully balanced. Typically, when a leader struggles, the root cause behind the nagging problem is the fact that the leader has steered off course. Awareness of the dichotomies in leadership permits this discovery, and thus enables the correction.

Made in the USA
Lexington, KY
30 January 2019